CONTRIBUTIONS FROM THE MUSEUM OF HISTORY AND TECHNOLOGY: PAPER 23

THE INTRODUCTION OF SELF-REGISTERING METEOROLOGICAL INSTRUMENTS

Robert P. Multhauf

The Introduction of SELF-REGISTERING METEOROLOGICAL INSTRUMENTS

Robert P. Multhauf

The development of self-registering meteorological instruments began very shortly after that of scientific meteorological observation itself. Yet it was not until the 1860's, two centuries after the beginning of scientific observation, that the self-registering instrument became a factor in meteorology.

This time delay is attributable less to deficiencies in the techniques of instrument-making than to deficiencies in the organisation of meteorology itself. The critical factor was the establishment in the 1860's of well-financed and competently directed meteorological observatories, most of which were created as adjuncts to astronomical observatories.

THE AUTHOR: *Robert P. Multhauf is head curator of the department of science and technology in the United States National Museum, Smithsonian Institution.*

The flowering of science in the 17th century was accompanied by an efflorescence of instrument invention as luxurious as that of science itself. Although there were foreshadowing events, this flowering seems to have owed much to Galileo, whose interest in the measurement of natural phenomena is well known, and who is himself credited with the invention of the thermometer and the hydrostatic balance, both of which he devised in connection with experimentation on specific scientific problems. Many, if not most, of the other Italian instrument inventors of the early 17th century were his disciples. Benedetto Castelli, being interested in the effect of rainfall on the level of a lake, constructed a rain gauge about 1628. Santorio, well known as a pioneer in the quantification of animal physiology, is credited with observations, about 1626, that led to the development of the hygrometer.

Both of these contemporaries were interested in Galileo's most famous invention, the thermoscope—forerunner of the thermometer—which he developed about 1597 as a method of obtaining comparisons of temperature. The utility of the instrument was immediately recognized by physicists (not by chemists, oddly enough), and much ingenuity was expended on its perfection over a 50-year period, in northern Europe as well as in Italy. The conversion of this open, air-expansion thermoscope into the modern thermometer was accomplished by the Florentine Accademia del Cimento about 1660.

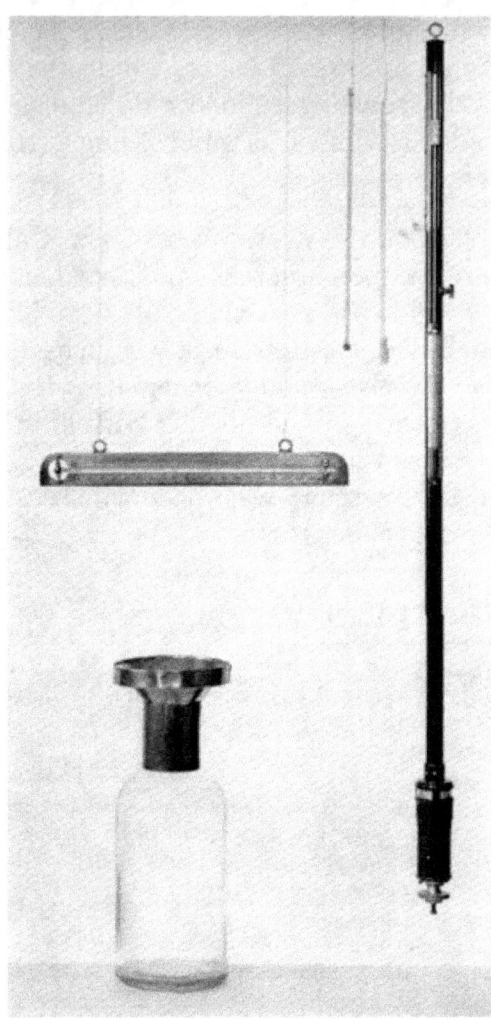

Figure 1.—A set of typical Smithsonian meteorological instruments as recommended in instructions to observers issued by the Institution in the 1850's. *Top* (from left): maximum-minimum thermometer of Professor Phillips, dry-bulb and wet-bulb thermometers, and mercurial barometer by Green of New York. *Lower left:* rain gauge. The wet-bulb thermometer, although typical, is actually a later instrument. The rain gauge is a replica.

Galileo also inspired the barometer, through his speculations on the vacuum, which, in 1643, led his disciple Torricelli to experiments proving the limitation to nature's horror of a vacuum. Torricelli's apparatus, unlike Galileo's thermoscope, represented the barometer in essentially its classical form. In his earliest experiments, Torricelli observed that the air tended to become "thicker and thinner"; as a consequence, we find the barometer in use (with the thermometer) for meteorological observation as early as 1649.[1]

The meetings of the Accademia terminated in 1667, but the 5-year-old Royal Society of London had already become as fruitful a source of new instruments, largely through the abilities of its demonstrator, Robert Hooke, whose task it was to entertain and instruct the members with experiments. In the course of devising these experiments Hooke became perhaps the most prolific instrument inventor of all time. He seems to have invented the first wind pressure gauge, as an aid to seamen, and he improved the bathometer, hygrometer, hydrometer, and barometer, as well as instruments not directly involved in measurement such as the vacuum pump and sea-water sampling devices. As in Florence, these instruments were immediately brought to bear on the observation of nature.

It does not appear, however, that we would be justified in concluding that the rise of scientific meteorology was inspired by the invention of instruments, for meteorology had begun to free itself of the traditional weather-lore and demonology early in the 17th century. The Landgraf of Hesse described some simultaneous weather observations, made without instruments, in 1637. Francis Bacon's "Natural History of the Wind," considered the first special work of this kind to attain general circulation, appeared in 1622.[2] It seems likely that the rise of scientific meteorology was an aspect of the general rationalization of nature study which occurred at this time, and that the initial impetus for such progress was gained not from the invention of instruments but from the need of navigators for wind data at a time when long voyages out of sight of land were becoming commonplace.

It should be noted in this connection that the two most important instruments, the thermometer and barometer, were in no way inspired by an interest in meteorology. But the observation made early in the history of the barometer that the atmospheric pressure varied in some relationship to visible changes in the weather soon brought that instrument into use as a "weather glass." In particular, winds were attributed to disturbances of barometric equilibrium, and wind-barometric studies were made by Evangelista Torricelli, Edmé Mariotte, and Edmund Halley, the latter publishing the first meteorological chart. In 1678-1679 Gottfried Leibniz endeavored to encourage observations to test the capacity of the barometer for foretelling the weather.[3]

Other questions of a quasi-meteorological nature interested the scientists of this period, and brought other instruments into use. Observations of rainfall and evaporation were made in pursuit of the ancient question of the sources of terrestrial water, the maintenance of the levels of seas, etc. Physicians brought instruments to bear on the question of the relationship between weather and the incidence of disease. The interrelationship between these various meteorological enterprises was not long in becoming apparent. Soon after its founding in 1657 the Florentine academy undertook, through the distribution of thermometers, barometers, hygrometers, and rain gauges, the establishment of an international network of meteorological observation stations, a network which did not survive the demise of the Accademia itself ten years later.

Not for over a century was the first thoroughgoing attempt made at systematic observation. There was a meteorological section in the Academy of Sciences at Mannheim from 1763, and subsequently a separate society for meteorology. In 1783, the Academy published observations from 39 stations, those from the central station comprising data from the hygrometer, wind vane (but not anemometer), rain gauge, evaporimeter, and apparatus for geomagnetism and atmospheric electricity, as well as data from the thermometer and barometer. The Mannheim system was also short-lived, being terminated by the Napoleonic invasion, but systems of comparable scope were attempted throughout Europe and America during the next generation.

In the United States the office of the Surgeon General, U. S. Army, began the first systematic observation in 1819, using only the thermometer and wind vane, to which were added the barometer and hygrometer in 1840-1841 and the wind force anemometer, rain gauge, and wet bulb thermometer in 1843. State weather observation systems meanwhile had been inaugurated in New York (1825), Pennsylvania (1836), and Ohio (1842).[4]

Nearly 200 years of observation had not, however, noticeably improved the weather, and the naive faith in the power of instruments to reveal its mysteries, which had possessed many an early meteorologist, no longer charmed the scientist of the early 19th century. In the first published report of the British Association for the Advancement of Science in 1833, J. D. Forbes called for a reorganization of procedures:

> In the science of Astronomy, for example, as in that of Optics, the great general truths which emerge in the progress of discovery, though depending for their establishment upon a multitude of independent facts and observations, possess

sufficient unity to connect in the mind the bearing of the whole; and the more perfectly understood connexion of parts invites to further generalization.

Very different is the position of an infant science like Meteorology. The unity of the whole ... is not always kept in view, even as far as our present very limited general conceptions will admit of: and as few persons have devoted their whole attention to this science alone ... no wonder that we find strewed over its irregular and far-spread surface, patches of cultivation upon spots chosen without discrimination and treated on no common principle, which defy the improver to inclose, and the surveyor to estimate and connect them. Meteorological instruments have been for the most part treated like toys, and much time and labor have been lost in making and recording observations utterly useless for any scientific purpose. Even the numerous registers of a rather superior class ... hardly contain one jot of information ready for incorporation in a Report on the progress of Meteorology....

The most general mistake probably consists in the idea that Meteorology, as a science, has no other object but an experimental acquaintance with the condition of those variable elements which from day to day constitute the general and vague result of the state of the *weather* at any given spot; not considering that ... when grouped together with others of the same character, [they] may afford the most valuable aid to scientific generalization.[5]

Forbes goes on to call for a greater emphasis on theory, and the replacement of the many small-scale observatories with "a few great Registers" to be adequately maintained by "great Societies" or by the government. He suggests that the time for pursuit of theory might be gained from "the vague mechanical task to which at present they generally devote their time, namely the search for great numerical accuracy, to a superfluity of decimal places exceeding the compass of the instrument to verify."

From its founding the British Association sponsored systematic observation at various places. In 1842 it initiated observations at the Kew Observatory, which has continued until today to be the premier meteorological observatory in the British Empire. The American scientist Joseph Henry observed the functioning of an observatory maintained by the British Association at Plymouth in 1837, and when he became Secretary of the new Smithsonian Institution a few years later he made the furtherance of meteorology one of its first objectives.

The Kew Observatory set a pattern for systematic observation in England as, from 1855, did the Smithsonian Institution in the United States. The instruments used differed little from those in use at Mannheim over half a century earlier[6] (fig. 1). They were undoubtedly more accurate, but this should not be overstressed. Forbes had noted in his report of 1832 that some scientists were then calling for a return to Torricelli, for the construction of a temporary barometer on the site in preference to reliance on the then existing manufactured instruments.

The First Self-Registering Instruments

From the middle of the 17th century meteorological observations were recorded in manuscript books known as "registers," many of which were published in the early scientific journals. The most effective utilization of these observations was in the compilation of the history of particular storms, but where a larger synthesis was concerned they tended, as Forbes has shown, to show themselves unsystematic and non-comparable. The principal problems of meteorological observation have been from the outset the construction of precisely comparable instruments and their use to produce comparable records. The former problem has been frequently discussed, and perhaps, as Forbes suggests, overemphasized. It is the latter problem with which we are here concerned.

The idea of mechanizing the process of observation, not yet accomplished in Forbes' time, had been put forward within a little over a decade of the first use of the thermometer and barometer in meteorology. On December 9, 1663, Christopher Wren presented the Royal Society with a design for a "weather clock," of which a drawing is extant.[7] This drawing (fig. 2) shows an ordinary clock to which is attached a pencil-carrying rack, geared to the hour pinion. A discussion of the clock's "reduction to practice" began the involvement of Robert Hooke, who was "instructed" in September 1664 to make "a pendulum clock applicable to the observing of the changes in the weather."[8] This tribute to Hooke's reputation—and to the versatility of the mechanic arts at this time—was slightly overoptimistic, as 15 years ensued before the clock made its appearance.

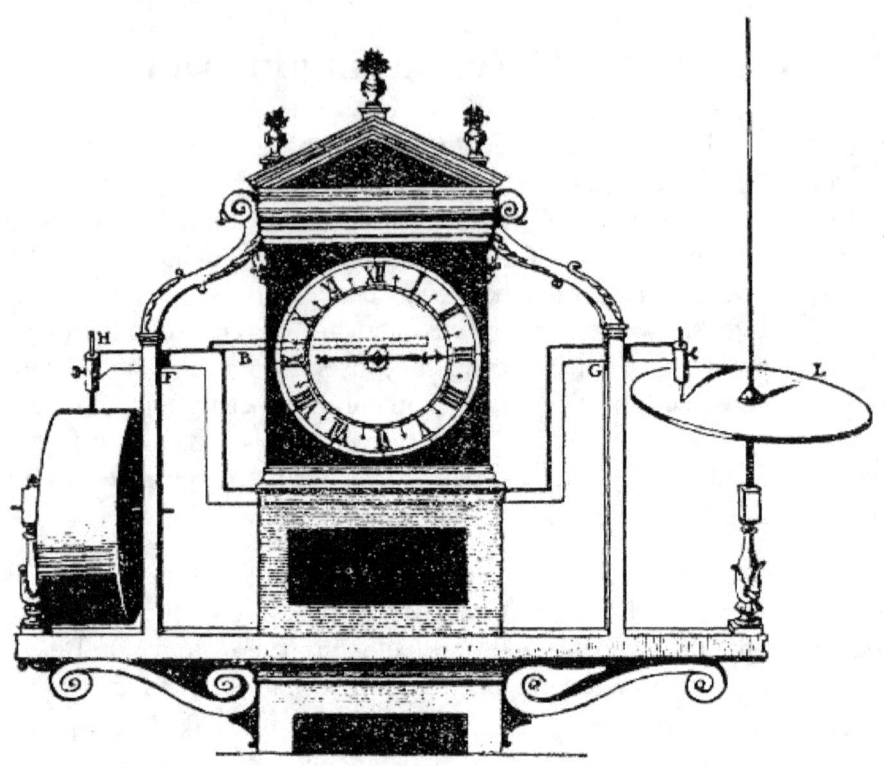

Figure 2.—A contemporary drawing of Wren's "weather clock." (Photo courtesy Royal Society of London.)

References to this clock are frequent in the records of the Royal Society—being mainly periodic injunctions to Hooke to get on with the work—until its completion in May 1679. The description which Hooke was asked to supply was subsequently found among his papers and printed by William Derham as follows:[9]

> The weather-clock consists of two parts; *first*, that which measures the time, which is a strong and large pendulum-clock, which moves a week, with once winding up, and is sufficient to turn a cylinder (upon which the paper is rolled) twice round in a day, and also to lift a hammer for striking the punches, once every quarter of an hour.
>
> *Secondly*, of several instruments for measuring the degrees of alteration, in the several things, to be observed. The first is, the barometer, which moves the first punch, an inch and half, serving to shew the difference between the greatest and the

least pressure of the air. The second is, the thermometer, which moves the punch that shews the differences between the greatest heat in summer, and the least in winter. The third is, the hygroscope, moving the punch, which shews the difference between the moistest and driest airs. The fourth is, the rain-bucket, serving to shew the quantity of rain that falls; this hath two parts or punches; the first, to shew what part of the bucket is fill'd, when there falls not enough to make it empty itself; the second, to shew how many full buckets have been emptied. The fifth is the wind vane; this hath also two parts; the first to shew the strength of the wind, which is observed by the number of revolutions in the vane-mill, and marked by three punches; the first marks every 10,000 revolutions, the second every 1,000, and the third every 100: The second, to shew the quarters of the wind, this hath four punches; the first with one point, marking the North quarters, viz. N.: N. by E.: N. by W.: NNE.: NNW.: NE. by N. and N.W. by N.: NE. and N.W. The second hath two points, marking the East and its quarters. The third hath three points, marking the South and its quarters. The fourth hath four points, marking the West and its quarters. Some of these punches give one mark, every 100 revolutions of the vane-mill.

The stations or places of the first four punches are marked on a scrowl of paper, by the clock-hammer, falling every quarter of an hour. The punches, belonging to the fifth, are marked on the said scrowl, by the revolutions of the vane, which are accounted by a small numerator, standing at the top of the clock-case, which is moved by the vane-mill.

What, exactly, were the instruments applied by Hooke to his weather clock? It is not always easy even to guess, because it appears that Wren was actually the first to contrive such a device and seems to have developed nearly as many instruments as Hooke. It might be supposed that Hooke would have adapted to the weather clock his wheel-barometer, introduced in 1667, but it also appears that Wren had described (and perhaps built) a balance barometer before 1667.[10] As to the thermometer, we have no evidence of original work by Hooke, but we do have a description of Wren's self-registering thermometer, a circular, mercury-filled tube in which changes in temperature move "the whole instrument, like a wheel on its axis."[11]

The hygroscope (hygrometer) probably existed in more versions than any other instrument, although we know nothing of any versions by Wren. Hooke may have used his own "oat-beard" instrument.[12] Derham follows his description of the clock—which has been quoted above—with a detailed description of a tipping-bucket rain gauge invented by Hooke and used with the clock. He also notes that in 1670 Hooke had described two other types of rain gauge in which a bucket was counterbalanced in one case by a string of bullets and in another by an immersed weight. But here again, Sprat records the invention of a tipping-bucket gauge by Wren before 1667.

Hooke has been generally regarded as the first inventor of an anemometer, in 1662.[13] But this invention was a pressure-plate gauge—that is, a metal plate held with its face against the wind—whereas the gauge used with the weather clock is clearly a windmill type, of which type this may be the first. Wren also had an anemometer, but we have no description of it. Hooke's account does not refer to other instruments which the weather clock is supposed to have had, according to a description quoted by Gunther, which concludes the enumeration of the elements recorded with "sunshine, etc."[14] One can only wish for further information on the mechanism by which the punches—or in Wren's clock, the pencils—were moved. But it is apparent that Hooke's clock was actually used for some time.

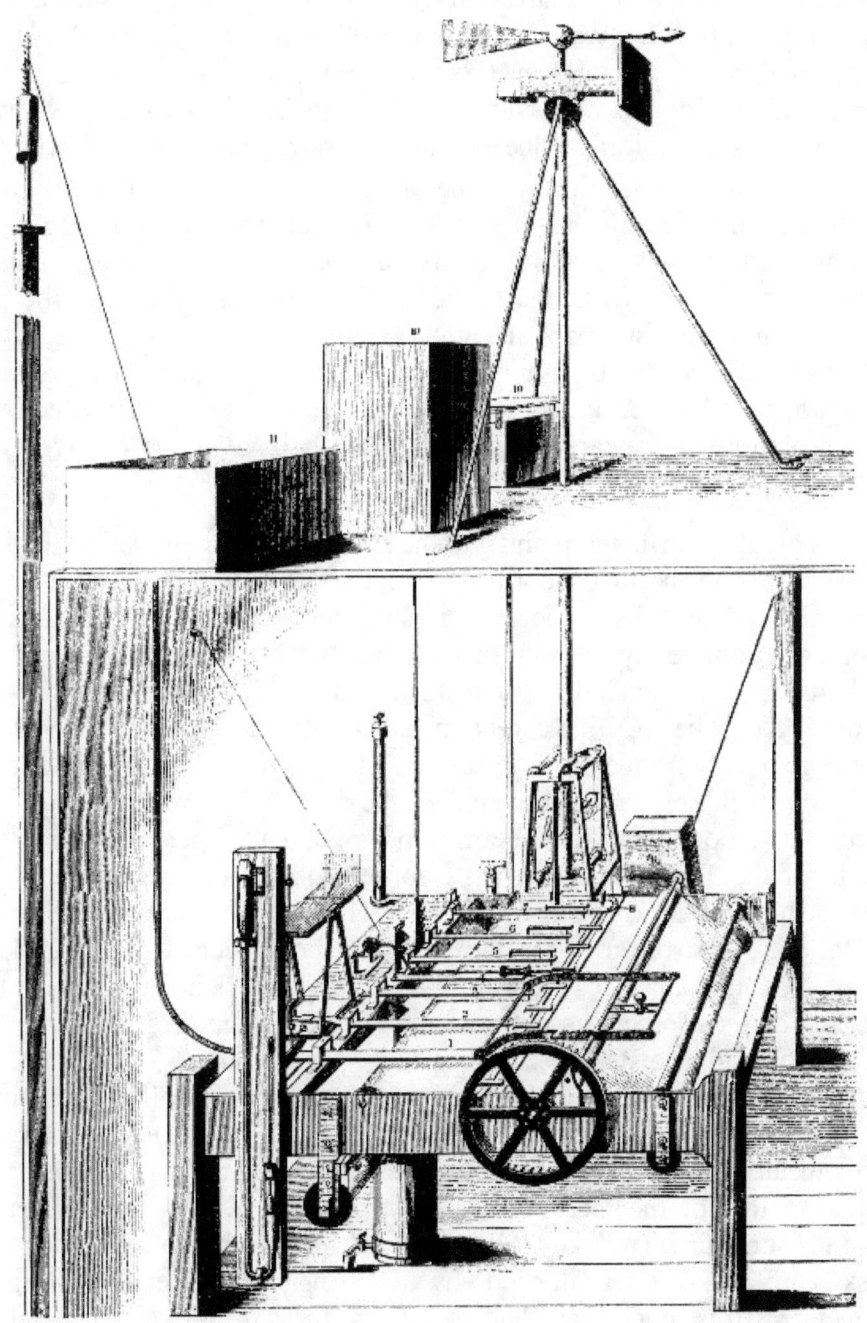

Figure 3.—Dolland's "atmospheric recorder": 1, siphon and float barometer; 2, balance (?) thermometer; 3, hygrometer; 4, electrometer; 5, float rain gauge; 6, float evaporimeter; 7, suspended-weight wind force indicator; 8, wind direction indicator; 9, clock; 10, receivers for rain gauge and evaporimeter. (From *Official ... Catalogue of the Great Exhibition, 1851*, London, 1851, pt. 2).

The 17th century was not entirely unprepared for the idea of such a self-registering instrument. Water clocks and other devices in which natural forces governed a pointer were known in antiquity, as were counters of the type of the odometer. A water clock described in Italy in 1524 was essentially an inversion of one of Hooke's rain gauges, that in which a bucket was balanced against a string of bullets.[15] The mechanical clock also had a considerable history in the 17th century, and had long since been applied to the operations of figures through cams, as was almost certainly the case with the punches in Hooke's clock. Still, the combination of an instrument-actuated pointer with a clock-actuated time-scale and a means of obtaining a permanent record represent a group of innovations which certainly ranks among the greatest in the history of instrumentation. It appears that we owe these innovations to Wren and Hooke.

Hooke's clock contributed nothing to the systematization of meteorological observation, and the last record of it appears to have been a note on its "re-fitting" in 1690. Its complexity is sufficient reason for its ephemeral history, but complexity in machine design was the fashion of the time and Hooke may have intended no more than a mechanistic *tour de force*. On the other hand, he may have recognized the desideratum to which later meteorologists frequently returned—the need for simultaneous observations of several instruments on the same register. In any case, no instrument so comprehensive seems to have been attempted again until the middle of the 19th century, when George Dolland exhibited one at the Great Exhibition in London (see fig. 3). The weather elements recorded by Dolland's instrument were the same as those recorded by Hooke's, except that atmospheric electricity (unknown in Hooke's time) was recorded and sunshine was not recorded. Striking hammers were used by Dolland for some of the instruments and "ever pointed pencils" for the others. Dolland's barometer was a wheel instrument controlling a hammer. His thermometric element consisted of 12 balanced mercury thermometers. Its mode of operation is not clear, but it probably was similar to that of the thermometer developed by Karl Kreil in Prague about the same time (fig. 4). Dolland's wind force indicator consisted of a pressure plate counterbalanced by a string of suspended weights. Altogether, it is not clear that Dolland's instrument was superior to Hooke's, or that its career was longer.[16]

The 171 years between these two instruments were not lacking in inventiveness in this field, but even though inventors set the more modest aim of a self-recording instrument for a single piece of meteorological data, their brain children were uniformly still-born. Then, during the period 1840-1850, we see the appearance of a series of self-registering instruments which were actually used, which were widely adopted by observatories, and which were superseded by superior instruments rather than abandoned. This development was undoubtedly a consequence of the establishment at that time of permanent observatories under competent scientific direction.

Long experience had demonstrated to the meteorologists of the 1840's that the principal obstacle to the success of self-registering instruments was friction. Forbes had indicated that the most urgent need was for automatic registration of wind data, as the erratic fluctuation of the wind demanded more frequent observation than any manual system could accomplish. Two of the British Association's observers produced separate recording instruments for wind direction and force in the late 1830's, a prompt response which suggests that it was not the idea which was lacking. One of these instruments—designed by William Whewell—contained gearing, the friction of which vitiated its utility as it had that of a number of predecessors. The other, designed by A. Follet Osler, was free of gearing; it separately recorded wind pressure and direction on a sheet of paper moved laterally by clockwork. The pressure element was a spring-loaded pressure plate carried around by the vane to face the wind. Both this plate and the vane itself were made to move pencils through linkages of chains and pulleys.[17] Osler's anemometer (fig. 5) deserves to be called the first successful self-registering meteorological instrument; it was standard equipment in British observatories until the latter part of the 19th century when it was replaced by the cup-anemometer of Robinson.

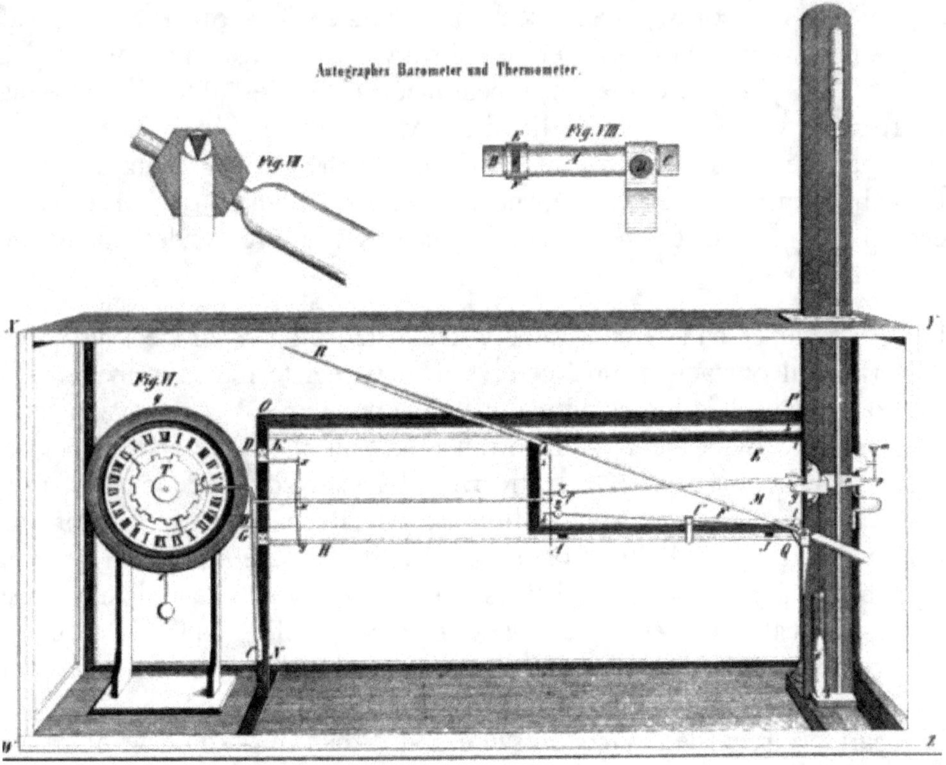

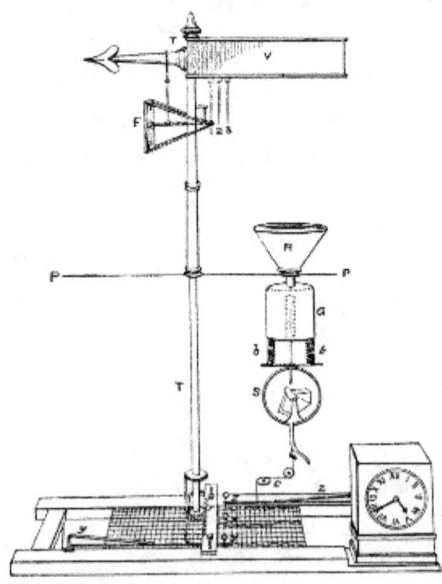

Figure 4.—Kreil's balance thermometer, 1843. (From Karl Kreil, *Magnetische und meteorologische Beobachtungen zu Prag*, Prague, 1843, vol. 3, fig. 1.)

Figure 5.—Osler's self-registering pressure plate anemometer, 1837. The instrument is shown with a tipping-bucket rain gauge. (From Abbe, *op. cit.* footnote 17.)

Self-recording barometers and thermometers were more vulnerable to the influence of friction than were wind instruments, but fortunately pressure and temperature were also less subject to sudden fluctuation, and so self-registration was less necessary. Nevertheless, two events occurred in the 1840's which led to the development of self-registering instruments. One event was the development of the geomagnetic observatory, which used the magnetometer, an instrument as delicate as the barometer and thermometer, and (as it then seemed), as subject to fluctuation as the wind vane. The other event was the development of photography, making possible a recording method free of friction. In 1845 Francis Ronalds at Kew Observatory and Charles Brooke at Greenwich undertook to develop apparatus to register the magnetometer, electrometer, thermometer, and barometer by photography.[18] This was six years after Daguerre's discovery of the photographic process. The magnetometers of both investigators were put into use in 1847, and the barometers and thermometers shortly after. They were based on the deflection—by a mirror in the case of the magnetometer and electrometer and by the mercury in the barometer and thermometer—of a beam of light directed against a photographic plate. Brooke exhibited his instruments at the Great Exhibition of 1850, and they subsequently became items of commerce and standard appurtenances of the major observatory until nearly the end of the century (fig. 6). Their advantages in accuracy were finally insufficient to offset the inconvenience to which a photographic instrument was subject.

Before 1850 the British observatories at Kew and Greenwich (the latter an astronomical observatory with auxiliary meteorological activity) had self-registering apparatus in use for most of the elements observed.

Self-Registering Systems

In 1870 the Signal Corps, U.S. Army, took on the burden of official meteorology in the United States as the result of a joint resolution of the Congress and in accordance with Joseph Henry's dictum that the Smithsonian Institution should not become the permanent agency for such scientific work once its permanency had been decided upon. Smithsonian meteorology had not involved self-recording instruments, and neither did that of the Signal Corps at the outset "because of the expense of the apparatus, and because nothing of that kind was at that time manufactured in this country."[19]

But almost immediately after 1870 the Signal Corps undertook an evidently well-financed program for the introduction of self-registration. "Complete outfits" were purchased, representing Wild's system, the Kew system as made by Beckley, Hipp's system (fig. 8), Secci's meteorograph (figs. 9, 10), Draper's system, and Hough's printing barograph and thermograph. Of these only the Kew system, the photographic system already mentioned, could have been obtained before 1867.

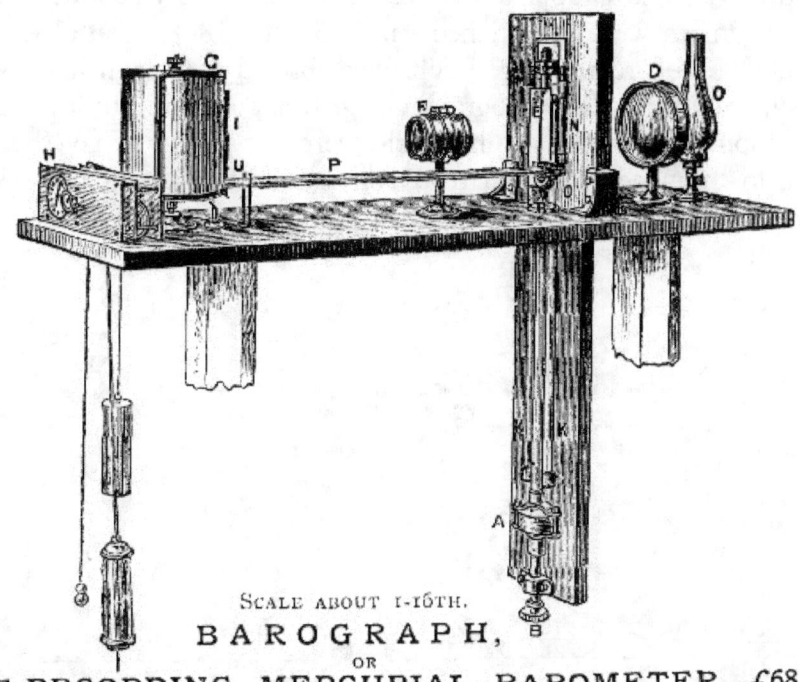

SCALE ABOUT 1-16TH.

BAROGRAPH,
OR
SELF-RECORDING MERCURIAL BAROMETER, £68.

Figure 6.—Photographic registering mercurial barometer, typical commercial version. (From J. J. Hicks, *Catalogue of ... Meteorological Instruments*, London, n.d., about 1870.)

Like Kew, Daniel Draper's observatory in Central Park, New York City, was established primarily for meteorological observation.[20] Draper was one of the sons of the prominent scientist J. W. Draper. Hipp was an instrument-maker of Neuchâtel who specialized in precision clocks.[21] The others after whom these "systems" were named were directors of astronomical observatories, which were, at this time, the most active centers of meteorological observation. Wild was at the Bern Observatory, [22] Secci at the Papal Observatory, Rome,[23] and George Hough at the Dudley Observatory, Albany, New York.[24] While the Signal Corps seems to have acquired all of the principal "systems," some interesting instruments were developed at still other observatories, notably by Kreil at the astronomical observatory in Prague.[25] The principal impetus for this full-scale mechanization of observation undoubtedly came from the directors of astronomical observatories.

Thus within little more than the decade of the 1860's were developed five new systems of meteorological self-registry that were sufficiently well thought of to be adopted or copied by observatories outside their places of

19

origin. Wild and Draper tell us that it was decided when their respective observatories were established—in 1860 and 1868—that all instruments should be self-registering. Each was obliged to design his own, being dissatisfied with the photographic registers commercially available. The development of these systems would therefore appear to have been due, in part, to the general spread of a conviction that satisfactory instruments were attainable.

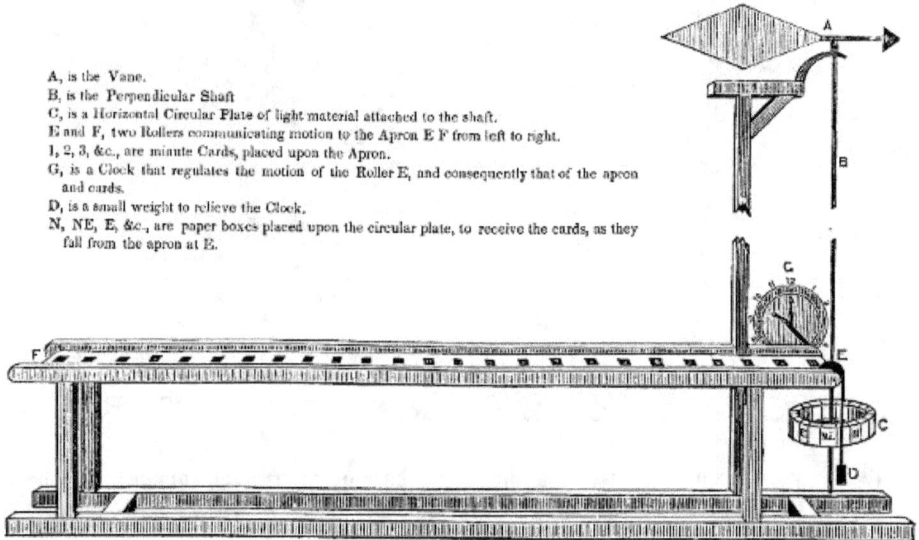

A, is the Vane.
B, is the Perpendicular Shaft
C, is a Horizontal Circular Plate of light material attached to the shaft.
E and F, two Rollers communicating motion to the Apron E F from left to right.
1, 2, 3, &c., are minute Cards, placed upon the Apron.
G, is a Clock that regulates the motion of the Roller E, and consequently that of the apron and cards.
D, is a small weight to relieve the Clock.
N, NE, E, &c., are paper boxes placed upon the circular plate, to receive the cards, as they fall from the apron at E.

Figure 7.—In 1838 the pioneer American meteorologist James H. Coffin (1806-1873) devised a self-registering wind direction indicator; in 1849 he improved it as shown here. The band, moved by clockwork, carries cards marked with the day and hour. In Coffin's earlier instrument, a part of which is now in the Smithsonian Institution, the vane carried a funnel for sand, which ran into a circular row of bottles. (From *Proceedings of the American Association for the Advancement of Science*, 1849, vol. 2, p. 388.)

This confidence was warranted, for the decade of the 1850's had seen the appearance of major innovations in the basic instruments—thermometer, barometer, and wind velocity indicator—that made available instruments more adaptable to self-registration. It also saw the development of a new method of electrical registration derived from the telegraph. Sir Charles Wheatstone initiated this small revolution in 1843 when he reported to the British Association that he had constructed an electromagnetic meteorological register which "records the indications of the barometer, thermometer and the psychrometer [meaning wet-bulb thermometer] every half hour ... and prints the results on a sheet of paper in figures," running a week unattended. The working of this register involved the insertion of a conductor in the tubes to make a circuit, the thermometers having open tops.[26] This was ten years after the development of the electromagnetic relay and six years after Wheatstone's introduction of his own telegraph.

Wheatstone's instrument left a very ephemeral record in the meteorological literature, and appears to have been defective or out of fashion with its time, which was concerned with the introduction of photographic instruments. Wheatstone's work was rediscovered, along with that of several other much earlier inventors, by the determined observatory directors of the 1860's.

Of the five systems developed at that time, four used electromagnetic registration, only Draper adhering to a mechanical system (see fig. 11). For temperature measurement Secci and Hough used Wheatstone's electrical system with a mercurial thermometer (fig. 12), but the other four utilized a physical principle which had been proposed periodically for at least a century—the unequal thermal expansion of a bimetallic strip. This principle had been utilized by watchmakers for a quite different purpose —the temperature compensation of the watch pendulum—but its possibilities as a thermometer had been known long before the mid-19th century.[27]

Figure 8.—Hipp's registering aneroid barometer, with a telegraphic printer.
(*USNM 314544; Smithsonian photo 46740-D.*)

For the measurement of pressure, Secci, Wild, and Draper adopted, or rediscovered, the balance barometer devised by Wren in the 17th century. In this type of instrument (see figs. 13, 15) either the tube or the reservoir of the barometer is attached to one arm of a balance, the equilibrium of which is disturbed by the movement of the mercury in the instrument.[28]

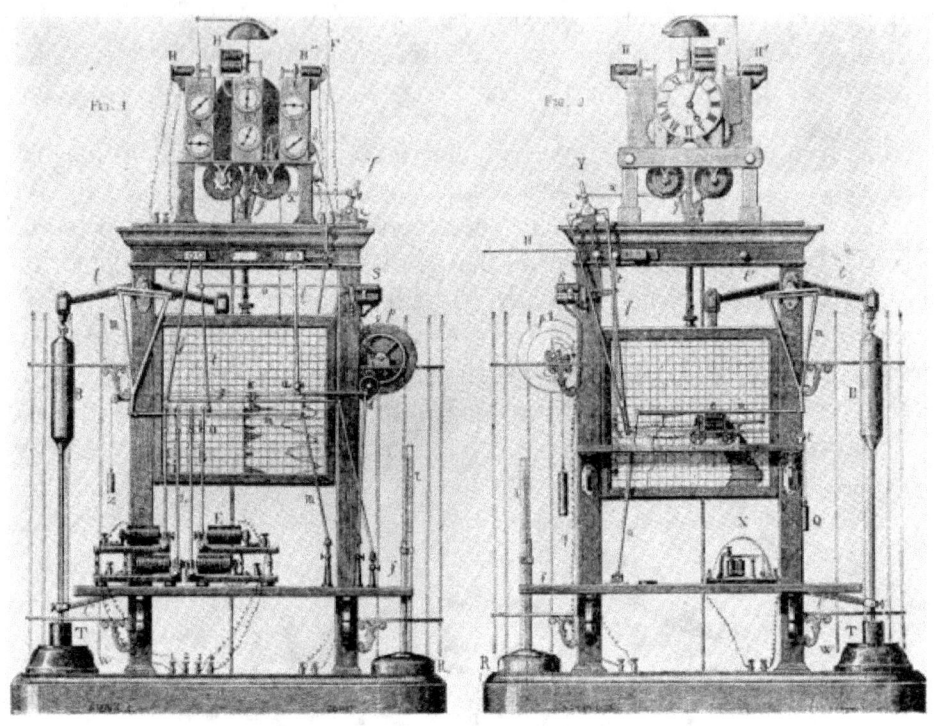

Figure 9.—Front and rear views of Secci's meteorograph, 1867. (From Lacroix, *op. cit.* footnote 22.)

Hough's barometer was an adaptation of the electrical contact thermometer. The movement of the mercury over a certain minute distance within the tube served as a switch to energize an electrical recording system. Hipp, who was perhaps the latest of this group, first applied the aneroid barometer (fig. 8) to self-registration. The idea of the aneroid—an air-tight bellows against which the atmospheric pressure would act—had been advanced by Leibniz in the 17th century and had been the subject of a few abortive experiments in the 18th century. Not until 1848 was an instrument produced that was acceptable to users of the barometer.[29]

As a wind velocity instrument all six systems used the cup-anemometer developed by Robinson in 1846, an instrument whose chief virtue was the care which its inventor had taken to work out the relationship between its movement and the actual velocity of the wind.[30] Beckley and Draper caused it to move a pencil through gearing; the others used with it electromagnetic counters actuated by rotating contacts.

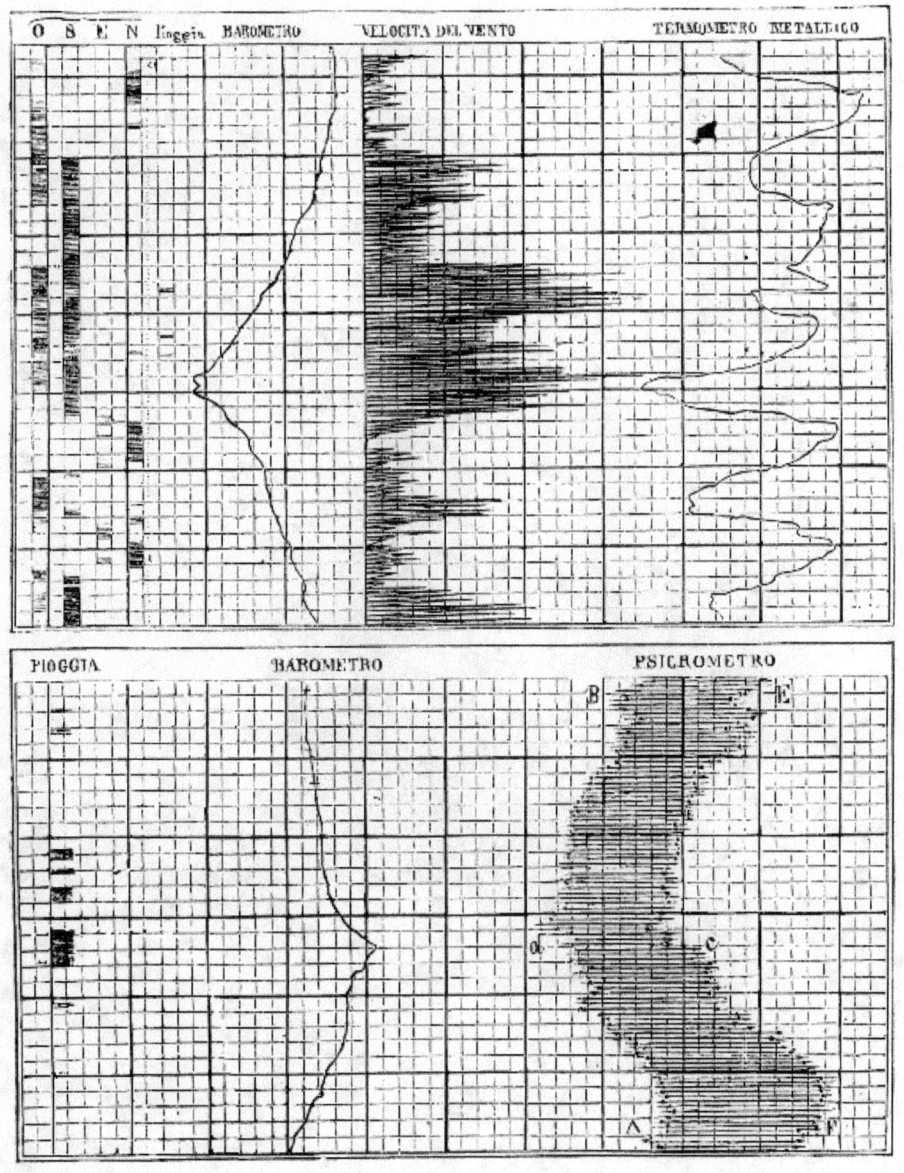

Figure 10.—Chart from Secci's meteorograph. (From Lacroix, *op. cit.* footnote 22.)

As has been indicated, the Signal Corps used all six systems, a panoply of gadgetry which must have been wondrous to behold. Its Secci meteorograph, which had attracted much attention at Paris, was estimated to have cost 15,000 francs. Abbe reported in 1894 that the instruments were long kept in the apparatus room "as a fascinating show to visitors and a stimulation to the staff in the invention of other instruments."[31]

Figure 11.—Draper's mechanical registering barometer, as used in the Lick Observatory. (Photo courtesy Lick Observatory.)

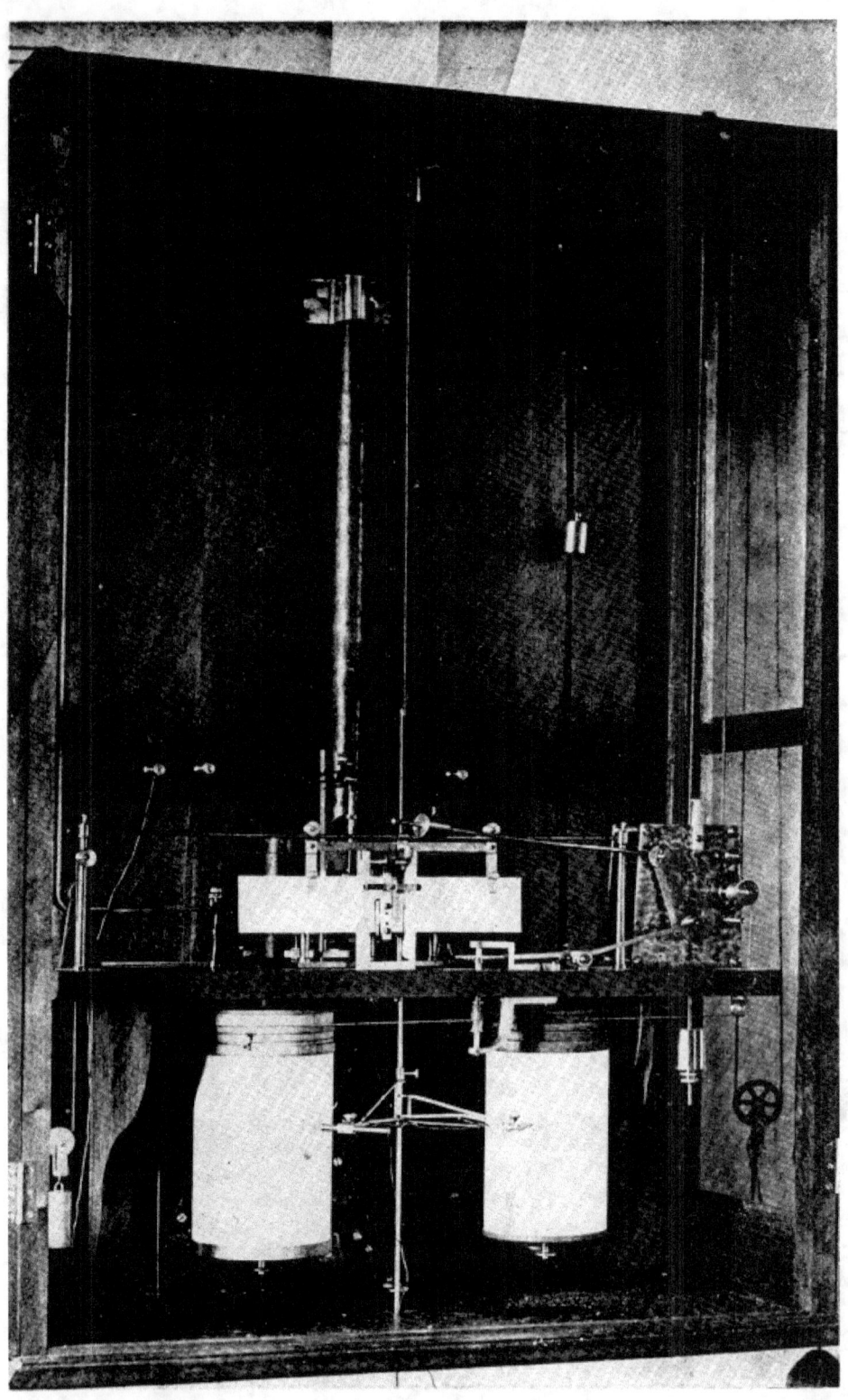

Figure 12.—Hough's electromechanical registering barometer, about 1871.

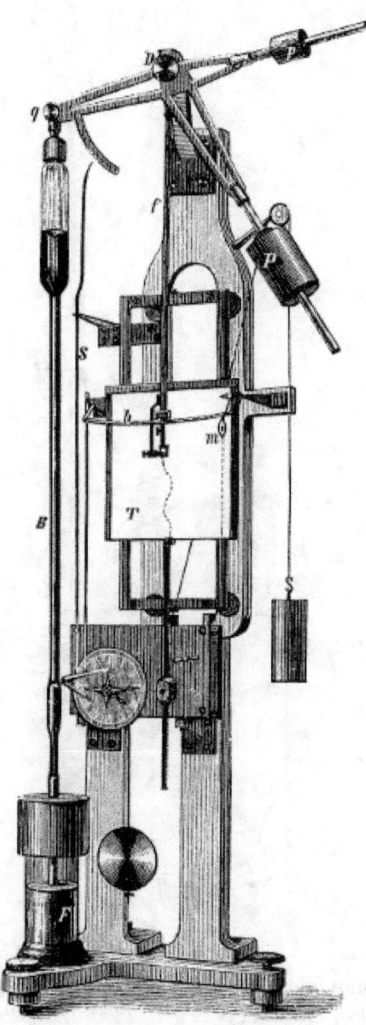

Figure 13.—Fuess' "balance barometer after Samuel Morland," 1880. Wren probably was the originator of this type of instrument. (From Loewenherz, *op. cit.* footnote 28.)

Figure 14.—Marvin's mechanical registering barometer, 1905. This instrument was formerly in the U.S. Weather Bureau. (*USNM 316500; Smithsonian photo 46740-E.*)

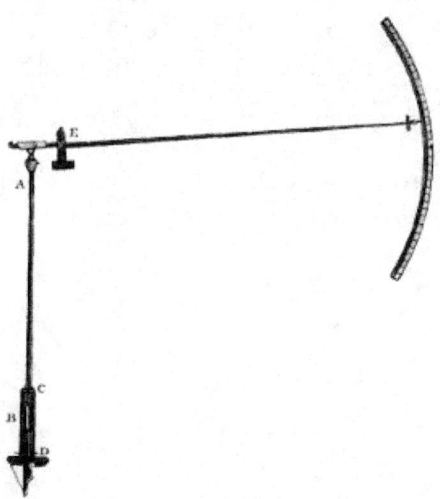

Figure 15.—"Steelyard barometer" as shown in Charles Hutton's *Mathematical and Philosophical Dictionary* (London, 1796, vol. 1, p. 188). Hutton makes no reference to the originator of this instrument; he attributes the "Diagonal" (or inclined) barometer to Samuel Morland.

From 1875 the question was no longer one of the introduction of self-registering instruments to major observatories but their complete mechanization and the extension of registration to substations. Having accepted self-registration, meteorologists turned their attention to the simplification of instruments. In 1904 Charles Marvin, of what is now the U.S. Weather Bureau, brought the self-registering barometer into something of a full circle by producing an instrument (fig. 14) that was nothing more than Hooke's wheel barometer directly adapted to recording. [32] But this process of simplification had been accomplished at a stroke, about 1880, with the introduction by the Parisian instrument-maker Jules Richard of a self-registering barometer and a thermometer combining the simplest form of instrument with the simplest form of registration (see fig. 16). This innovation, which fixed the form of the conventional registering instrument until the advent of the radiosonde, seems to have stemmed from a source quite outside meteorology—the technology of the steam gauge. Richard's thermometric element was the curved metal tube of elliptical cross-section that Bourdon had developed several decades earlier as a steam gauge. Pressure within such a tube causes it to straighten, and thus to move a pointer attached to one end. Bourdon had opened it to the steam source. Richard filled it with alcohol, closed it, and found that the expansion of the alcohol on heating caused a similar straightening. His barometric element was a type of aneroid, which Hipp had already used but which Richard may have also adopted from a type of steam gauge. For a recording mechanism, Richard was able to use a simple direct lever connection, as the forces involved in his instruments, being concentrated, were not greatly hampered by friction.[33] By 1900 these simple and inexpensive instruments had relegated to the scrap pile, unfortunately literally, the elegant products of the mass attack of observatory directors in the 1860's on the problem of the self-registering thermometer and barometer.[34]

Conclusions

In view of the rarity of special studies on the history of meteorological instruments, it is impossible to claim that this brief review has neglected no important instruments, and conclusions as to the lineage of the late 19th century instruments can only be tentatively drawn. The conclusion is inescapable, however, that the majority of the instruments upon which the self-registering systems of the late 19th century were based had been proposed and, in most cases, actually constructed in the 17th century. It is also evident that in the 17th century at least one attempt was made at a system as comprehensive as any accomplished in the 19th century.

Figure 16.—Richard's registering aneroid barometer, an instrument used at the U.S. Weather Bureau about 1888. The Richard registering thermometer is similar, the aneroid being replaced by an alcohol-filled Bourdon tube. (*USNM 252981; Smithsonian photo 46740-C.*)

To attribute the success of self-registering instruments in the late 19th century to the unquestionable improvements in the techniques of the instrument-maker is to beg the question, for it is by no means clear that the techniques of the 17th-century instrument-maker were unequal to the task. It should also be noted that the photographic and electromagnetic systems of the 19th century seem to have been something of an interlude, for some of the latest and most durable (all of Draper's and Richard's instruments and Marvin's barograph) were purely mechanical instruments, as had been those of Hooke and Wren. If we conclude that the 19th-century instruments were more accurate, we should also recall Forbes' comments upon the question of instrumental accuracy.

What, then, was the essential difference between the 17th and 19th centuries that made possible the development of the self-registering observatory? It would appear to have been a difference of degree—the maturation in the 19th century of certain features of the 17th. The most important of these features were the spread throughout the western world of the spirit that had animated the scientific societies of Florence and London, the continued popularity of the astronomical observatory as an object of the philanthropy of an affluent society, and the continued existence of the nonspecialized scientist. Under these circumstances such nonmeteorologists as Wheatstone, Henry, Hough, Wild, and Secci had the temerity to range over the whole of the not yet compartmented branches of science and technology, fully confident that they were capable of finding thereby a solution to any problem important enough to warrant their attention.